How to B
a Chan

GW01465712

By Herb Welch

Foreword by "Dr. D" David Schultz

FOREWORD

I met Herb when he was 65 years old. I had never even seen wrestling before the day I went to his house and asked him to train me, but Herb saw something in me and agreed to work with me for $300.

Herb and I worked out three times a week. Herb would stretch me every night. He'd stretch me so bad, my wife would have to help me out of the car when I got home. I'd take a hot bath, my wife would put liniment on me, and the next day, I'd go set up six-foot high chain link for eight hours.

After a few weeks, I got used to it, and Herb began to bring in some other guys to work with me. They were real stiff, and they beat me up pretty bad.

Finally, one day Herb pulled me aside. "David," he said, "You need to forget everything I've taught you."

"Why?" I asked.

"Because if you work that way in the ring, no one will want to wrestle you or book you. You're going to hurt somebody!"

"What about these guys you've brought in?"I asked. "They are trying to hurt me!"

"They are doing what they do to protect themselves and the business," said Herb. Back then, the old timers wanted to push anyone who was not tough enough to drop out and give up on becoming a pro.

What I didn't realize was that Herb was teaching me how to shoot - how to wrestle and hurt people for real. "One day," he said, "Someone will get in the ring and test you. Then, you can use the things I taught you. You'll only have to do it once, and they'll learn to back off and respect you."

After that, Herb started over. He taught me how to work easy, how to work without hurting other people. Not that I was the easiest guy to work with. When you see me throw a punch, I'm throwing a punch. But I learned how to be a good worker, and I learned how to shoot well enough I could protect myself. And yes, I had to shoot on a few people.

Before Herb passed away, his widow Reba gave me a book Herb had put together of photos and instructions for various wrestling holds. It's a manual on how to shoot wrestle. All the stuff no one teaches anymore. This is what Herb taught me in those first few weeks, the lost art of how to shoot. Reba gave me permission to do with the book as I pleased, and John Cosper convinced me to share it with the wrestling world.

The book you hold in your hands is the kind of thing the fans were never meant to see. It's a peek behind the curtain of a bygone era. This is real wrestling history.

- "Dr. D" David Schultz

2017

Notice I have the left arm under the opponent's left arm and and back of the neck, forcing his head to the mat. Catch the right wrist with your right hand and pull. When you have it secured behind his back, push forward. I like to hook his left leg with my right leg to prevent him from turning.

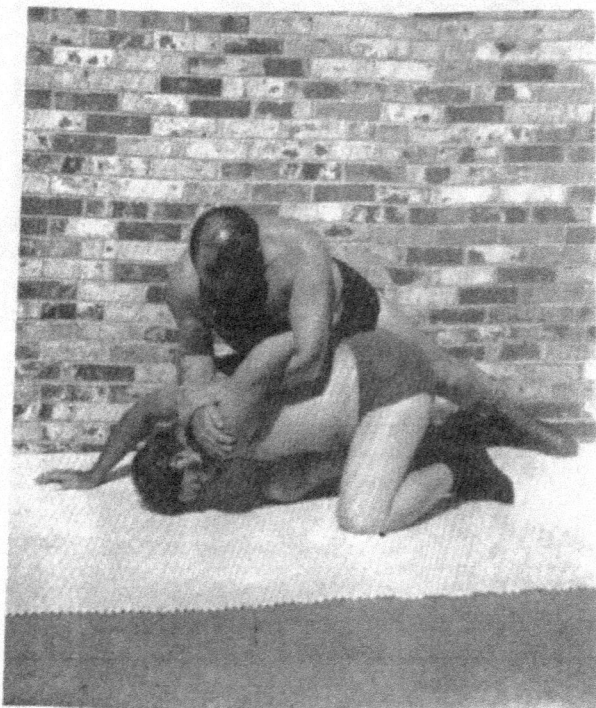

This is a very good hold from this position. Notice how I have my arm hooked, and bear down on the neck with the right elbow.

This is in the Nelson Family. As there are several different types of Nelsons, this is a good way to wear your opponent down. Sometimes it will win the match for you.

This is a good hold when you have your opponent down on the mat. Grab his left wrist with your left hand and push it behind his back. Reach over with your right hand under his right arm and around the neck, forcing his head to the mat. Notice how I have my right leg hooked over his left leg to prevent him from turning.

This hold is almost the same, except the arm is straight out and pushed forward. Be sure to hook the left leg with your right to prevent him from turning.

You can break a leg with this hold. From a hand and knee position, lie across the top of your opponent. Hook your right leg under his right leg. Fall off the right side and grab the toe with both hands. That is all she wrote.

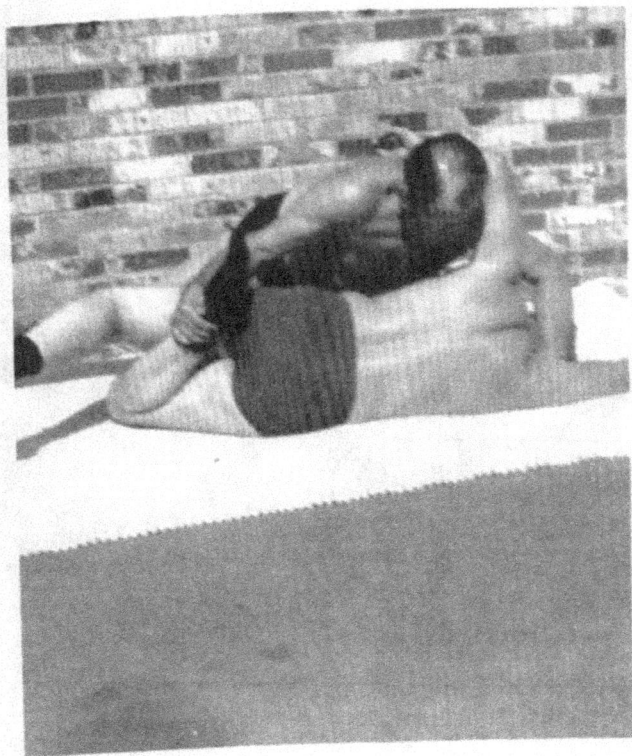

This is going for a pin. Catch the right leg with the right hand and hook the head as in this position. Turn him on his back for a pin.

This front face lock is a good way to damage your opponent's neck. This will take some of the fire out of him.

This is a good way to come out from under the bottom. Hook the left arm with your left arm, turning it into a hammerlock. Be sure and hook the left leg with your left leg to prevent him from turning over.

13

This is a dangerous hold. You have the left arm hooked with your legs, and both hands on his right arm. Then someone must give.

This is the old time hook sizzler and face lock. I have had
ribs broken with this hold.

This is a good way to throw your opponent to the mat.

This is a form of a ride — just to wear your opponent down.

This is the abdominal stretch. It has been used by more wrestlers than any other hold because it is a sure one once you get it applied.

This picture shows a hold, that once it is applied as I have it
here, the match may be yours very shortly.

This is a wristlock, and it is tough on the elbow. It is a hold every policeman should know.

This is an arm bar. I often used it to win a match.

This old crab hold has injured more backs for wrestlers than any other hold.

This one leg crab is almost as severe as the crab itself.

This is a type of Nelson. A strong armed man once gets it applied just right, and it's plain murder.

You get this hold from a flying mare. While your opponent
is still on his back, jump between his legs, grab both feet —
one in each hand — and then rear back.

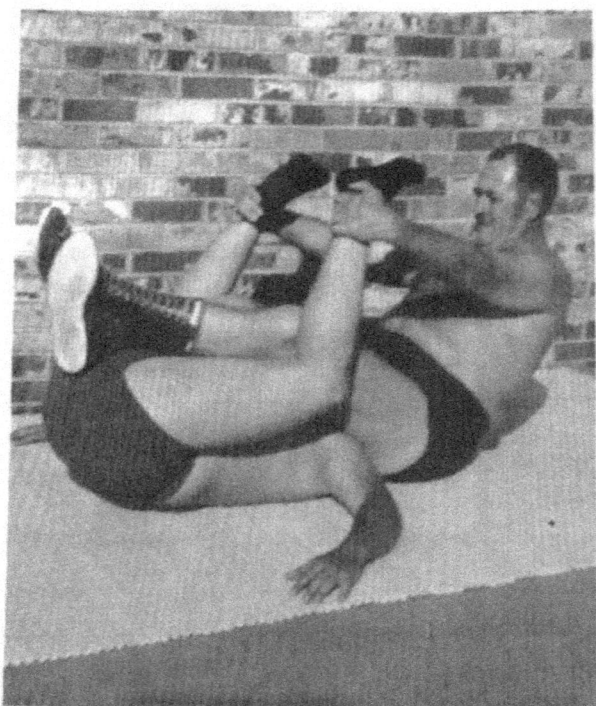

This picture shows it is better to go all the way back on the mat sometimes, still holding both feet.

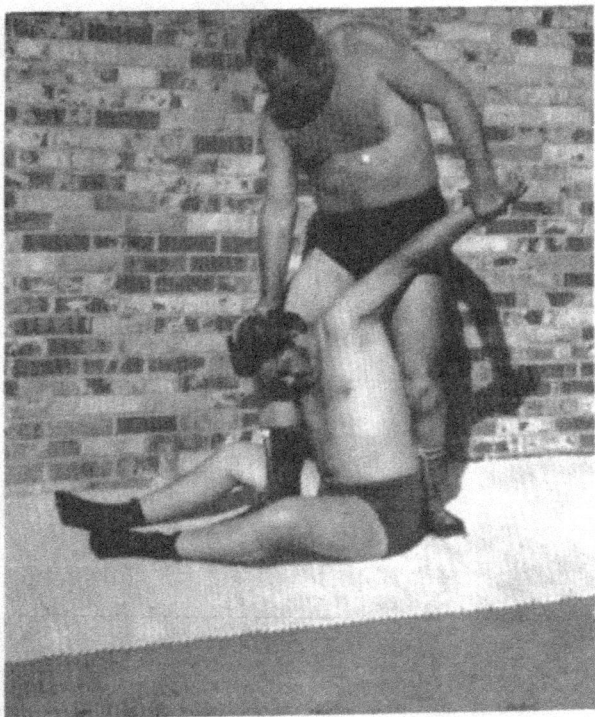

This hold speaks for itself. His left arm is barred and his right leg is blocked to prevent him from turning. Then push his head forward.

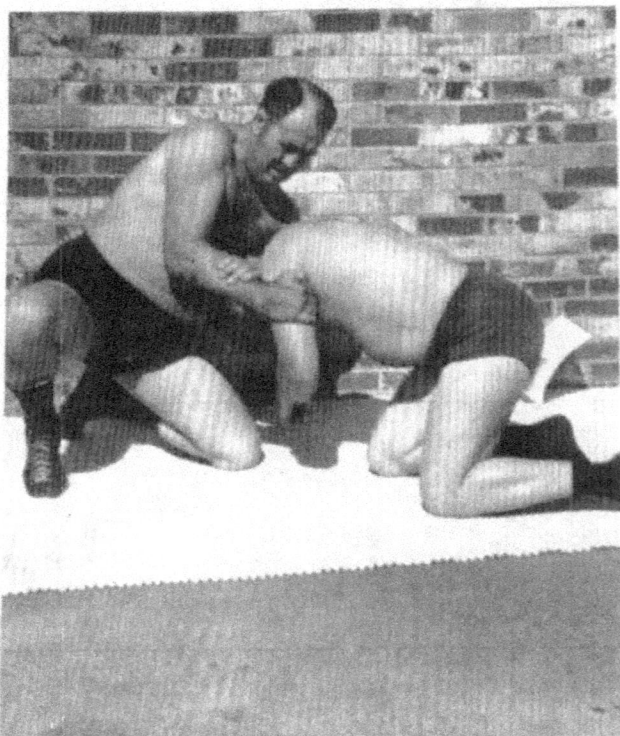

This front face lock and arm is death, once you get it applied
just right.

Catch the arm of your opponent, pulling him forward. Slip
in between his legs. With your other hand throw him over
your back. Then you can go to work.

This is an arm bar and face lock combined. It makes a terrific give up hold.

This is a hammer lock in early stage. Once you get this far along, there are quite a number of moves to make from here.

This is a pile driver hold. It is barred in almost every state. However, it is used sometimes. There have been a number of wrestlers hurt permanently with it.

This back breaker is also a very dangerous hold. You pick a man up, as in the picture, and drop him across the knee with the small part of his back. Most of the time this is it.

This hold is so severe that once you get it applied, your opponent will have to give up.

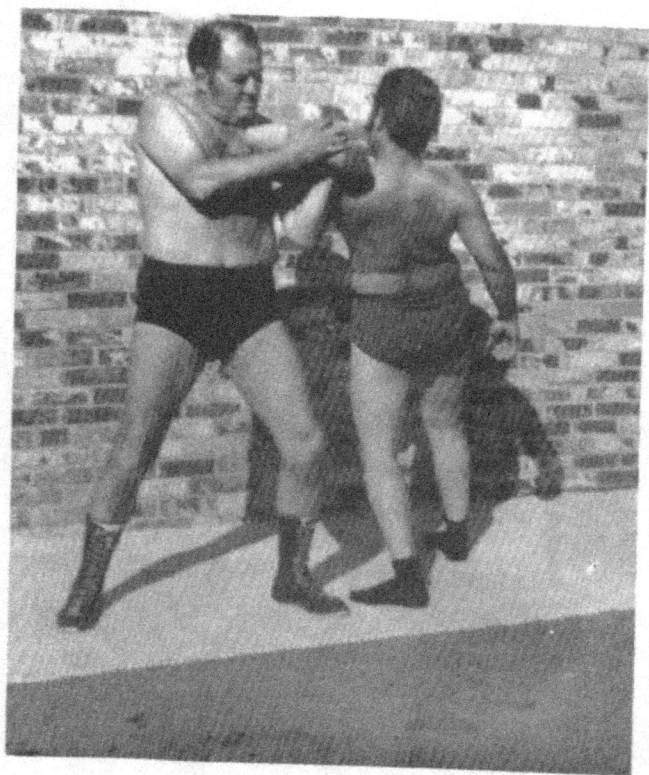

This is a standing wristlock most commonly used by all wrestlers.

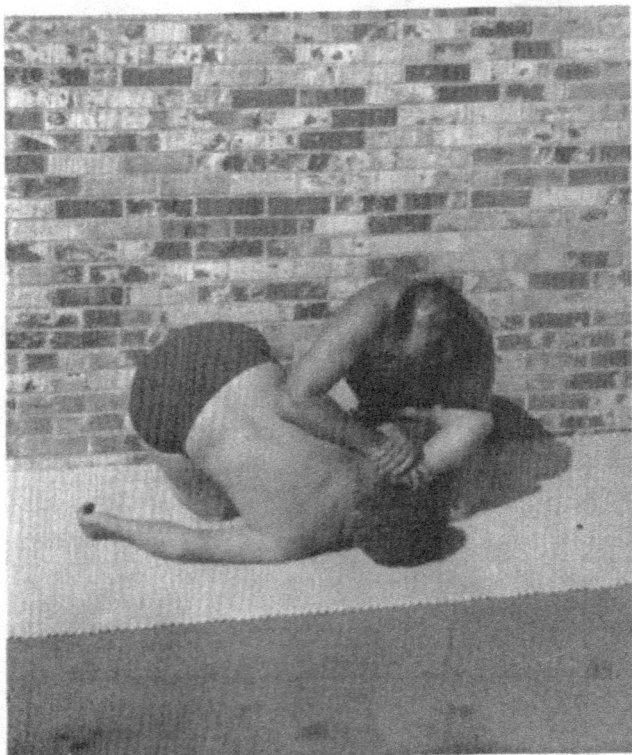

This is the beginning of a hammerlock. Once you have
applied this hold and forced your opponent to the mat,
you have almost won the match.

This hold works from a stepover toe hold. You move around and catch the opposite leg as shown in the picture. Bear down. This is a pin, as well as a painful stepover toe hold.

This is a double toe hold from a standing position.

A full Nelson is used to weaken a man. A man with long and strong arms has a good chance of forcing his opponent to submission.

This is a half abdominal with the left arm in a bad position. The right leg hooked by my right leg prevents him from turning.

This is a halfway tumbleweed. Both legs crossed over with toes hooked behind my legs. A good thing to do is to sit down on his back.

This is the hold that I have won many matches with. At that time I had strong legs and that is just what it takes. I could hold a man much longer, forcing him to submission. This is called my "Oklahoma" tumbleweed.

About the Author —

Herb Welch has wrestled professionally for 34 years during which time he has held the Southern Junior Heavyweight title four times and has been co-holder of the Southern Tag Team Championship five times. He has wrestled practically every "name" wrestler during this period. Before turning "pro" in 1938, he wrestled as an amateur for seven years.

★ ★ ★

An older brother, Roy Welch, introduced Herb to wrestling. He's now co-promotor with Nick Gulas in Memphis, Nashville, Birmingham, Chattanooga, Knoxville, and Louisville.

★ ★ ★

Besides Roy (who wrestled professionally for 30 years), Herb has two other brothers who have been or are still wrestlers: Lester, the youngest of the brothers, still wrestles and lives in Tampa, Fla., and Jack, who wrestled for 20 years before leaving the ring. He now lives in Huntsville, Ala., where he is in the construction business.

CPSIA information can be obtained
at www.ICGtesting.com
Printed in the USA
LVHW091417240121
677345LV00004B/819

9 781093 129250